YOU & YOUR CHILD

I.C.T. and computers

First published 1999

Letts Educational
Aldine House
Aldine Place
London W12 8AW
Telephone 020 8740 2266

Author: Ian Wilson
Series editor: Roy Blatchford
Consultants: Fay Turner and Graham Peacock
Project manager: Alex Edmonds
Editorial assistance: Tanya Solomons

Design by Peter Laws
Illustrations by Madeleine Hardy
Cover design by Peter Laws

British Library Cataloguing in Publication Data
A CIP record for this book is available at the British Library.

ISBN 185758 9793

Colour Reproduction by PDQ Repro Limited, Bungay, Suffolk.
Printed and bound in Italy

Letts Educational is the trading name of BPP (Letts Educational) Ltd

Letts Educational would like to thank all the parents who sent in their tips for educating children and who wrote with such enthusiasm about parenthood.

YOU & YOUR CHILD
I.C.T. and computers

Ian Wilson

Consultants: Fay Turner and Graham Peacock

Contents

Chapter One	What is I.C.T?	6
Chapter Two	Key Stage One (5 – 7 year olds)	10
Chapter Three	Key Stage Two (7 – 11 year olds)	14
Chapter Four	I.C.T. and special needs	18
Chapter Five	Buying a computer	20
Chapter Six	Setting up your computer	28
Chapter Seven	Buying software	32
Chapter Eight	Getting started	36
Chapter Nine	The Internet	46
Chapter Ten	Safety first	56
Glossary and Useful information		60

Words in **bold** are defined in the glossary at the back of this book.

"Do not confine your children to your own learning for they were born in different time."

HEBREW PROVERB

Dear Parent,

What happens at nursery and in primary school is vital to your child's education. What you do at home is just as important.

It's never too soon to start supporting your child's learning. The time that you spend with your child during the primary years gives him or her a foundation that will last a lifetime. Make the most of every opportunity for you and your child to enjoy learning together.

You don't need to be an expert. You do need to be enthusiastic. The time you invest at home – sharing activities at the computer, helping with homework, talking about projects – will help your child achieve all through primary and secondary school.

This book is one in a major new series from Letts. It will help you support your child, with information about how children use computers and technology at school. It explains the basics of word processing, spreadsheets, databases and using the Internet, and advises on choosing the best software to help your child progress.

I hope you enjoy sharing computing with your child. The important thing is to make learning fun!

Roy Blatchford.

ROY BLATCHFORD
Series editor

What is I.C.T?

I.C.T. stands for Information and Communications Technology. It covers the range of technological 'tools' that are used to process information – most often computers.

I.C.T. is the term that replaces I.T. (Information Technology). This is because many machines, such as telephones, TVs and fax machines, can be used to communicate with other people and machines, as well as to retrieve information. For example, you can now connect some mobile phones to computers to send and receive information and you can get onto the **Internet** via digital TV sets. As technology changes, such machines will be used to communicate information in even more ways.

Why is I.C.T. important?

I.C.T. is used everywhere, both as a channel for communication, and a means of processing information. Think about a typical day. You watch the weather forecast on TV. A computer has been used to prepare it, and produces the effects on the screen. You need money to go shopping so you get cash from a 'hole in the wall', which is linked to your bank's computer. A machine linked to a computer scans your purchases at the supermarket. You want to check the sports results – you use the **Ceefax** or **Teletext** service on your television screen. Videos and books can be stored on CDs, and banking can be done down the telephone or through the Internet.

All these technologies, and others which will be developed in the future, changing our daily lives. For children, I.C.T. will become more and more crucial for participating in the world around them. Children need to understand:

- ✔ the importance of I.C.T. in our work and society
- ✔ how to use I.C.T. for learning and problem-solving

Parent tip

"I don't have a computer, but I tried pointing out to my child where computers were being used, and soon he was thinking of more examples than me!"

I.C.T. and the National Curriculum

Schools aim to give pupils the opportunity to apply and develop their I.C.T. skills in various subjects. The **National Curriculum** states that 'I.C.T. capability is characterised by an ability to use effectively I.C.T. tools and information sources to analyse, process and present information, and to model, measure and control external events.'

Most schools will have computers for children to use, either in small groups or individually, usually supervised by a teacher. It is worth investigating your child's school policy on this. Many primary schools have computer rooms with a bank of networked (linked) computers that can be used with whole or half classes. Different subjects will encourage children to explore different uses of the technology.

THIS MAY INVOLVE:

- ✔ writing, drawing pictures or making models as part of Design Technology
- ✔ creating simple graphs in maths using spreadsheets
- ✔ drafting pieces of writing and changing these on the screen

I.C.T. in the home

Even if you don't have a computer at home, you can still support your child in his or her use of I.C.T. by communicating interest and helping to relate I.C.T. to the outside world. If you do have a computer available, you can encourage your child to use it for homework as well as for games. The key is to lead by example: if you are interested and willing to learn, your child will be too.

Parent quote

"When my child is doing homework on the computer, I ask her to explain to me what she's doing – that way I feel more comfortable with computers, and she has to think about what she's doing."

How you can help

- Find out how computers are used in schools, and how they can be used at home.

- You don't need to be an expert! You probably already support your child with reading and maths. You can use many of the same general techniques with I.C.T.

- Speak to your child's teacher about how the school uses computers, and what your child is learning. Your child's school may have a particular policy regarding the use of computers in homework.

- Encourage your child to experiment with I.C.T., and to practise his or her skills. This will help to improve the quality of his or her work. Make sure children understand any information they print off from a CD or the Internet. A computer printout alone is not what is usually required for a homework task.

Computers are particularly useful for children who need:

- to communicate without speech
- non-sighted methods of reading
- technological aids in practical and written work
- aids or adapted equipment to allow access to practical activities.

More information on I.C.T. and special needs can be found in Chapter Four.

The National Grid for Learning

The government are very keen to develop the use of I.C.T. in schools and at home. They have set up the National Grid for Learning (NGfL) to help teachers and parents. You can find information about I.C.T. and links to other useful websites by logging onto the NGfL site on the Internet (see Chapter Eleven). The web address is: www.ngfl.gov.uk

The other websites listed on the NGfL have been carefully checked to make sure that they are safe for children, and of a high quality.

The intention is that eventually the NGfL will be the place to find out about education courses and to link up with other people interested in all aspects of learning. At the end of this book you will find some more addresses and useful information.

Parent tip

"Make sure your child still does his or her work – I worry that my children do so much on computers that they're forgetting how to write!"

Key Stage One (5-7 year olds)

During Key Stage One your child will be learning to use I.C.T. at school for specific purposes. He or she will gain confidence and discover that computers can be very useful tools in schoolwork and fun learning. Your child will learn to become familiar with **hardware** and **software**, as he or she develops ideas and records work using I.C.T.

YOUR CHILD WILL LEARN:

- ✔ about different kinds of information and how they are presented
- ✔ how to find and share information in different ways
- ✔ to explore a variety of I.C.T. tools
- ✔ about the uses of I.C.T. inside and outside school

USING EQUIPMENT

Although some pre-schools now use computers, most children will be introduced to using computers in Key Stage One. They will learn basic skills like using a **mouse** or tracker ball to click on objects. They may operate computers in different ways.

- some computers have special keyboards with pictures
- ✔ some computers will 'speak' instructions and explanations to children through the loudspeakers

Basic skills learned in the classroom can be improved by using a computer. Your child can be introduced to letters and sounds through a computer **program**, for instance by tracing the letter shape with a tracker ball and hearing how it sounds through the speakers.

With a simple painting or drawing program your child can practise making marks of different colours and textures on the screen. This supports your child's creative development.

Sorting objects can be done on screen – for instance, your child might be asked to click on all the red objects. The computer can then congratulate your child when he or she gets it right! This supports your child's learning in maths.

Language activities

Word bank programs enable teachers to set up a screen displaying several words. The child chooses the word he or she wants and uses the mouse to click on it. The chosen word then moves onto the part of the screen where the child is assembling his or her work. If the child is writing about his or her family the following words might be available:

me, my, the, mummy, daddy, brother, sister, cat, dog, and, house, live

These can be assembled into sentences:

My mummy and daddy and the dog live with me. My sister lives with me.

Some schools use other input devices, called **concept keyboards**, which are large pads connected to the computer. The teacher programs the computer so that when a word or picture on the pad is pressed the corresponding word appears in the child's writing on screen.

There are many ways that computers can be used to develop your child's writing skills. For example teachers and parents can help more experienced Key Stage One children to experiment with stories using computers.

Teachers or parents can prepare half-finished stories for a child to complete. Stories with mistakes in them are fun for children to correct, using the Delete key, and then inserting the correct text. In this case the adult has made clear which words need changing by making them bold:

Parent quote

"Tanya writes lots of stories on our computer. We're going to keep them so that she can look back on them in years to come."

THE THREE BEARS

There were once **two** bears who lived in a wood. There was Mummy Bear, Daddy Bear and Baby Bear. Daddy Bear made some **cornflakes** but they were too **cold** to eat. They went for a walk until the porridge was **hot** enough to eat. Along came Goldilocks who was a little **boy** with **black** hair.

Children can save the writing, perhaps in their own computer file, and then change the saved version later. An exercise such as this can be a lot of fun if two children work on it together. The discussion between children when working on any computer programme is one of the more important ways in which I.C.T. promotes learning.

First activities in I.C.T.

- Children will create stories before they are able to write by moving pictures around to tell their own stories. This helps to prepare them for reading and writing by giving them a good sense of how stories are put together.

- Children may be asked to collect information about their environment, for example, 'How do we get to school?'. They will learn how to use a computer to record this information, and produce graphs or charts. They will learn how to sort the information and how to make simple predictions based on it.

- Children will also use programs that give them practice in skills like learning their tables or spellings. These programs are designed to give children lots of practice without repeating exactly the same questions. The programs often record all the children's attempts and results so that the teacher can see how they are progressing.

Control and turtles

An important part of what children need to learn is how computers control other things. For example, a computer chip controls modern washing machines and video recorders.

A **turtle** is like a little robot on wheels. It may be attached to the computer by a cable or it might be radio-controlled. Children learn how to tell the turtle what to do. They learn how to enter a sequence of commands on screen (forward, back, turn right etc.) that control the turtle. One of the computer languages often used for this is called **Logo**.

Some skills your child will develop during Key Stage One:

- ✔ Recognising simple symbols, such as Play and Stop.
- ✔ Learning how to enter and store information in a variety of forms.
- ✔ Describing what he or she has done on a computer and what happened.
- ✔ Programming a floor turtle using simple instructions in the right order to carry out a task.

Key Stage Two (7–11 year olds)

During Key Stage Two, pupils will extend the range of I.C.T. tools that they use, and develop their skills of enquiry. They will start to decide for themselves how and when to use computers. They will be able to choose which is the best program to use for a particular purpose. They will begin to judge where to find information and what they then need to do with it!

This is the most demanding part of the curriculum during this Key Stage, because collecting information is fairly easy. Real learning happens when children organise and choose from the information they have gathered.

Parent quote

"We found that Tony loved writing stories on the computer. He'd never really shown much interest in writing before, but the computer seemed to really help him."

Some skills your child will develop during Key Stage Two

At Key Stage Two children will develop the skills they acquired in Key Stage One. They will also learn some new ways of using a computer and other machines. Children will be working with I.C.T. in three areas that often overlap:

- communicating
- handling information
- control and modelling

COMMUNICATING

Children will use wordprocessors in more exciting ways. They are likely to use features such as spell checkers. They will learn about different forms of information such as:

- ✔ text
- ✔ sound
- ✔ graphics
- ✔ video

They will learn to choose from a range of programs for each type of information – for example, drawing packages as well as wordprocessors. They will learn how to move items from one package to another – for example how to move a picture from a drawing program into a wordprocessor. They will begin to use **desktop publishing** programs to produce professional-looking pieces of writing and might even learn how to create a web page.

WRITING

Teachers often find it difficult to persuade children that their writing could be improved or corrected. With a wordprocessor, this becomes easier. Children can move words, sentences and paragraphs around and try using different words as well as keeping different versions of a piece of writing to see which works best.

Parent tip

"Do make sure your child saves his or her work. The number of times we've lost something that's taken us hours to work on. It really is frustrating."

HANDLING INFORMATION

At Key Stage Two, children will begin to use databases to store information. For example, they might create a **database** that records all the 'favourites' of the class – colours, pets, teams, pop groups and so on. They will then learn how the information can be sorted in different ways. Your child could use the information in this database to produce graphs and tables. How many children in the class like the colour orange *and* have goldfish? There are endless combinations to explore. Children will also start to learn how to use **spreadsheets**, perhaps to record pocket money. Spreadsheet programs are very useful tools for encouraging children to develop their mathematical skills.

CONTROL AND MODELLING

We saw in Chapter Two how children learn to make a turtle or a robot carry out simple commands. Now they will learn how to create patterns of commands, especially patterns that can be repeated. By doing this, they learn to think logically and to understand the importance of getting things in the right order.

Another important skill is learning to ask (and answer) questions like 'What would happen if...?' Spreadsheets can be particularly good for this. There are also programs which are models. For example, a program might re-create what happens when a house is built. Children can experiment with the model and see the effects of their decisions – this is a lot easier on the computer than trying it in the playground.

Saving work

At Key Stage Two your child should be taught a routine for saving work in his or her own folder. Once a version has been saved, he or she can use the editing facilities of the wordprocessor to improve it. Your child should be encouraged to edit his or her work on screen and then print it out. The printed version can then be shown to the teacher and friends who might suggest changes before a final version. Changes that are easily made include:

Spelling
This can be checked automatically, but a spellcheck program usually misses apostrophes and words like their and there.

Layout of the work
The title can be centred and important words put in bold.

Appearance
A variety of fonts can be used to add interest.

I.C.T. and special needs

When I.C.T. is used properly it can help with children's learning. It can help teachers to identify where a child needs more support, and computer programs can act as patient tutors. Computers can help children with special needs to cover the same work as other children, but at their own pace. In this way, such children feel less 'different' from others, and can sometimes succeed in their use of computers where they struggle elsewhere.

Parent tips

"If your child has special needs, ask the school if there is any computer program they could use which would help. Sometimes it works, but doesn't occur to them unless you ask!"

"My child's school didn't know of any good programs for slow learners in numeracy. I found out about one through a friend and suggested the school buy it – they did."

Special equipment

A child with special needs does not necessarily need special equipment. Sometimes he or she can use different versions of the program (or software) being used, or begin at a different level or stage. However, some children will need to use equipment which helps them to communicate with the computer. For example, there are special keyboards which do not have keys. Instead they have large areas which the child can press. These concept keyboards can have a variety of sheets laid on them for use with different programs. For example, one sheet might have pictures of everyday objects, and another will have large words. Alternatively, a child might need to have all the instructions 'spoken' by a computer, either through headphones or the computer's speakers.

Teaching Programs

Teaching programs – software used in school to aid classwork – can be used with children of all abilities, but they can be particularly useful with children who need to learn at a slower pace. Sometimes these children can become discouraged when a teacher corrects them. Instruction and help from a computer can be far easier to accept – the child can sense how her or she is progressing, and feel in control of the learning experience. These programs can be used at home and in the school.

Helping with Literacy

The computer can help children overcome problems with literacy. Here are some examples:

1. Your child is frightened to write in case he or she gets the spelling wrong. A concept keyboard containing large words is used – your child can fill the gaps in a story by choosing and pressing the right word on the keyboard.
2. Your child is given a list of words on the computer. He or she copies these on the screen by typing them in. Any new words can be spoken, by the computer, so your child can learn through sight, sound and touch.
3. Your child can create his or her own story. A writing program can display various possibilities for a beginning, middle and end, which your child reads and accepts or rejects!

Integrated Learning Systems

There are now some very good programs – called integrated learning systems (ILS) – which help children to learn English, maths and science. These contain teaching material and exercises. The teacher shows the child where to start at a point in the program which suits the child's ability. The child works through the material and does the exercises. The next pieces of work which the computer gives the child are based on the results of how well they have coped with the first exercises, and so on. The computer keeps a record of each child's progress, enabling the teacher to see where additional help is needed. Children using these programs for a short time each day have shown considerable achievement. No child would be expected to work solely in this way, however, as talking with the teacher and classmates are also important elements in learning.

Parent tip

"There are sometimes computer courses for children at local community centres or YMCAs. If they are available, they're often worth it – my child's confidence in his schoolwork has increased dramatically from doing one."

Buying a computer

If you don't have a computer at home, you may have considered buying one, but been put off by the complication or expense. A home computer is not a necessity. Children will almost certainly have access to computers at school, and if not, they can be found easily in public libraries, some 'Internet cafés' and even in large toystores.

Parent tip

"Don't be fooled into thinking that you need the flashiest computer on the market. Ours is a very basic model and it serves us perfectly."

Despite this, there are still lots of very good reasons to think about buying a computer. I.C.T. is becoming an increasingly important part of society and our daily lives. This is reflected in the National Curriculum, which emphasises the role of I.C.T. in communication and information. Children will benefit more and more from having access to a computer, for their homework, enjoyment and personal and educational development.

Children are not the only ones who will use the computer. Some PC s (personal computers) are particularly designed for family use, and are worth considering as a family investment. Prices are perhaps not as high as you would expect, and will continue to fall. Older machines are perfectly adequate for most purposes and are frequently given away by businesses. It might be worth writing to a local large company to see if this is the case. Alternatively, this chapter will give you some pointers for looking into the possibility of buying.

Before you buy

There are hundreds of computers available now, but only a few decisions that need to be made before buying one.

WHAT SORT DO YOU WANT?

Your first decision is what sort of computer you would like. There are two main sorts of computer: a PC (personal computer) and a Mac (Apple Macintosh). The main difference is the way they operate. What you see on the screen, and some of the commands, are different.

- PCs are the sort most frequently used at home. There are hundreds of companies producing them – you may have heard of Compaq, Dell, Packard Bell, Gateway or Tiny, for instance.

- Macs are widely used in publishing and the media. The Mac is easier to use, and sometimes its machines are more colourful, but the range of software available to use on it is different from the more common PC software your child may use at school.

The bigger the better?

The bigger the numbers the more powerful the computer is. But don't feel you have to buy one that is 'top of the range'. Computer technology is changing rapidly – find something that suits your needs, and if necessary you can increase the capability of your computer ('upgrade' it) later. This may not necessarily be too expensive.

If you would like to have Internet access and email, you'll need at least 8Mb of RAM (memory) and a processor of 486MHz or faster. If you want to use some of the more complicated CD-Roms or a large variety of programs, you'll need at least 64Mb of RAM. (See page 22 for explanations of some of these terms.)

WHAT SPECIFICATION DO YOU NEED?

Specification refers to how large or powerful the various parts of the computer are. Just as when you buy a car you have a choice of engines and parts, so with a computer you need to decide what you need. Don't be scared of the jargon!

Parent quote

"At first I was terrified by all the computer jargon, but once I had heard it explained it was far more simple to decide what I wanted."

PROCESSOR

The processor is the part which controls your computer – the big metal box containing all the tricks. The processor has a speed, and this varies depending on how powerful it is. Look for the number of MHz (megahertz). The higher this is, the quicker the processor will be able to start programs and retrieve information. In other words, the bigger the number, the faster the computer.

HARD DISK

The hard disk stores all the programs you use, for example Microsoft Word, as well as all the work you do. The size is usually in gigabytes (Gb). 2Gb is the minimum you should consider. If the hard disk size is in megabytes (Mb) it will be too small!

RAM

The RAM is the memory of the computer. When you are actually using the computer it is the memory which holds what you are doing. Just as a child's desk needs to be big enough to hold all their books, papers and dictionaries, so the RAM needs to be able to hold all the documents he or she will create and use. If it is too small, you may not be able to run some programs. 32 Mb is a reasonable size, and 64Mb even better.

MULTIMEDIA

A multimedia computer can play sound and video, as well as still pictures. It is almost essential for a computer which will be used by a child. The computer will need:

> **Parent tip**
>
> "It's worth getting a lot of memory (RAM) on a home computer, because children want to be able to access more and more from it, and there needs to be room available."

★ A sound card.
This is fitted into the computer so it can produce sounds.

★ Speakers.
These can be separate, like those on a large stereo, or built in.

★ A CD-ROM drive.
A CD-ROM is a disk which looks like a music CD, but also contains words, sounds and pictures (still, moving, or both).

MODEM

A modem connects your computer to your telephone line so that you can use the Internet (see Chapter 9). Modems can be internal (built into the computer case) or external (plugged onto the side). When you use a modem to connect to the Internet you are using your telephone line in the same way you do to make a telephone call. This means that using the Internet generally costs the same as a local call – so the quicker you can get the information you need, the better! It is definitely worth considering the fastest modem available. This way you can:

★ cut your phone bill by connecting quickly
★ 'surf' the net and find information more efficiently

Where to buy

There are three main ways to buy a computer: from a retail store, from a dealer or through mail order.

1) A RETAIL STORE

High street stores and superstores, such as PC World or Byte, can be the easiest way to buy a computer.

Pros:

- You will be able to try out the machine or see a demonstration.
- You will almost certainly be able to take the computer home that day.
- You will know where to go if something goes wrong or doesn't work!

Cons:

- The range of computer makes and brands may be limited.
- Staff may have limited knowledge, or be trying to 'push' particular brands.

2) A DEALER

A local specialist in computers may carry a range of computer types, or only one. Dealers often sell 'own brands' assembled for them using different parts and makes. They can be found through local stores or advertisements.

Pros:

- The quality of advice is likely to be high.
- 'Own brand' computers can be very good value for money.

Cons:

- The variety of computers available may be limited.
- You may need a certain level of technical knowledge in order to check that 'own brand' machines are built from reliable parts.

Buying a printer

There is a huge range of printers available, varying from inexpensive black and white ones (which can take up very little room on a desk) to industrial quality colour laser jets. Your child is likely to want a colour printer – but it does not necessarily have to be the fastest on the market. You will probably need the following with your printer:

- ✔ software to load it up – probably a disc or CD-ROM
- ✔ cartridges for black or coloured inks
- ✔ A4 blank paper!

All these are easily available from a computer retailer, electrical store or stationers.

Remember to take into account the space you have available at home for a printer!

3) MAIL ORDER

Many specialist computer magazines carry adverts from mail order companies. Some of the larger companies also advertise regularly in national newspapers. As with dealers, some companies only sell their 'own brand' machines.

Pros:

- The computers usually cost less that those sold in shops.
- You can often order specific requirements for your computer – for instance, the amount of memory and size of hard disk you would like.

Cons:

- You can't try the machine before you buy!
- Reliability of companies can vary. Check, for example, how long it will take to deliver the computer after your cheque has been cashed!
- There may be expensive delivery costs, particularly if your machine needs repair.

Parent quote

"I was surprised how simple it is to add things on to our computer. We started with basic word programs – now we can play videos!"

Then there's the extras:

The bits and pieces which connect to the computer are called peripherals. The main ones – which all computers must have – are the monitor (screen), keyboard and mouse. Most people will also buy a printer. Other peripherals include:

- **Scanner**

This scans (copies) pictures, photographs or even pages of text and transfers them onto your screen so you can change or alter them.

- **Digital Camera**

This looks like an ordinary camera, but instead of taking photos on a film, it stores them electronically so that they can be loaded onto your computer. Once the photos are in your computer, you can use them in other programs (for instance, putting a photo of your child in a homemade card), print them out, or store them.

- **Joystick**

This looks a bit like the gearstick on a car, and is used in many computer games to control what happens on screen.

Questions to ask

WHAT SERVICE DOES THE SHOP/DEALER PROVIDE?

Some retailers will come to your home and set up the machine for you. There may be an extra charge for this.

HOW GOOD IS THE WARRANTY?

★You may have difficulties with your computer – it may even break. Will you have to return the computer to the shop or dealer (return to base) or will the repairs be carried out in your home (on-site)?

★ Check how many years the warranty is valid for. Are both parts and labour covered? Can you extend the period of the warranty? Beware – some dealers may sell an extended warranty on poor terms. You might do better to buy one from the manufacturer, your credit card company or firms which cover domestic electrical goods.

HOW EASY IS IT TO UPGRADE?

To upgrade means to put in new parts which are faster/larger/better than the ones you originally had. For instance, you may find after two years that your hard disk is full of programs and data, and decide to put in a larger disk. It is worth checking how long it would take to add new memory, for instance. Unless you really know what you are doing, do not attempt to add new parts yourself!

Parent tip

"I think it's best to go somewhere where the staff really know what they are talking about – especially if, like me, you don't really know what it's all about."

WHAT SOFWARE WILL RUN ON THIS COMPUTER?

- ✔ If there is a particular program or piece of software you want to use, ask if it will run on the computer you are considering. The minimum specifications will be on the software box.
- ✔ Some computers come with software 'bundled' or 'thrown in' with it. Do not let this sway your decision, especially if you are unlikely to use all of the bundle!

CAN I ADD OTHER PARTS AND PERIPHERALS?

You will almost certainly want to add a printer, and this will be no problem. But you might also want to add, now or later, a scanner, digital camera or joystick. Check that there will be enough **ports** (sockets) for all these peripherals.

ARE MANUALS AVAILABLE?

The machine will come with some books (manuals) telling you how to use it. But not all the software which is already built in will necessarily have manuals. Dealers often put software on the computer before you buy it ('pre-load') – you may have to pay separately for manuals for this. It is also worth asking about disks for this pre-loaded software. That way, if the software fails for any reason, you can always reload it yourself.

Setting up your computer

Once you've bought a computer, setting it up in your home can seem a daunting task. Don't forget that some shops or dealers offer to set up the whole system for you at your home. They may well charge for this. Alternatively, you can try it yourself – the instructions here should make it an easy process!

Parent tip

"Make sure you've got the computer set up near power points, otherwise you'll have cable all over the place."

Your computer will look something like this:

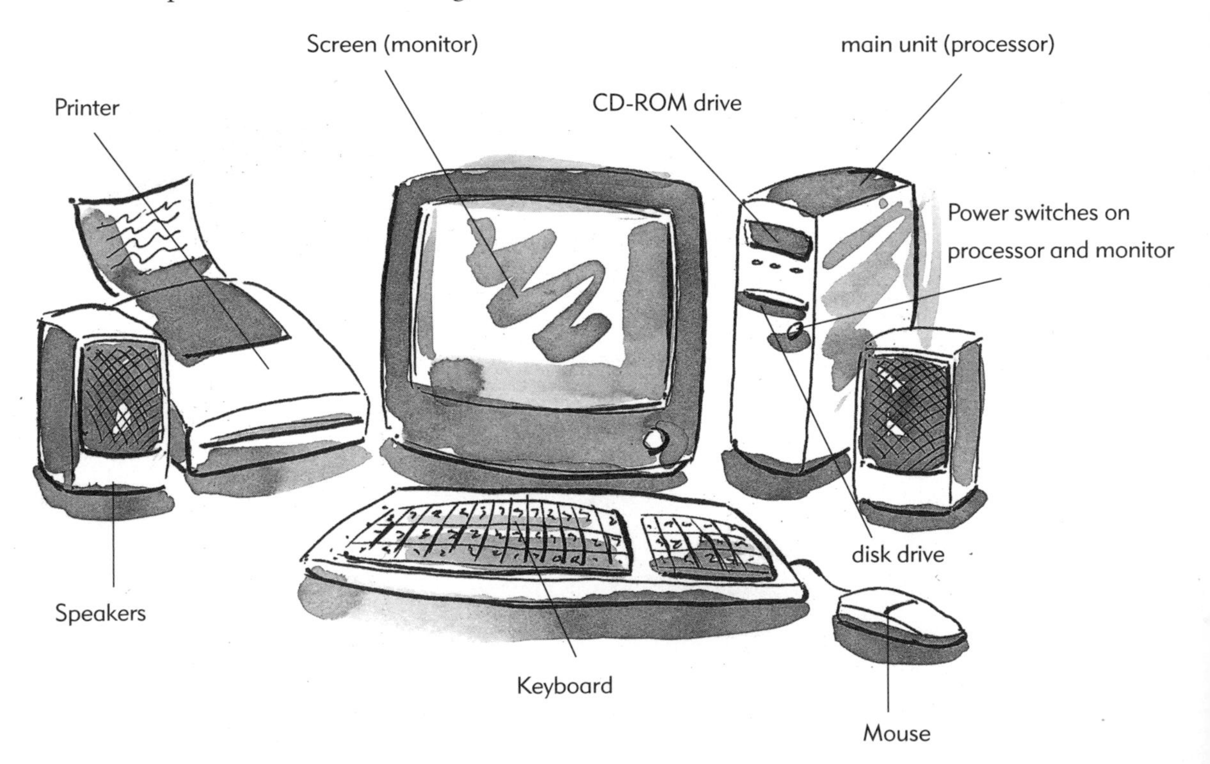

Plugging In

The surge protector

Our electricity supply can sometimes have a surge – like a large wave (most obviously in the advertisements breaks of a major sporting event on television, when half the country turn their kettles on). These surges can damage the delicate parts inside your computer. A surge protector or line filter is a special kind of plug which prevents the surge from reaching your computer. You can buy one from any electrical retail store, or from a computer retailer – they will explain how to fit it into the mains plug.

1 Unpack all the boxes carefully. Keep the packaging and boxes – you will need them if you have to send anything back for repair.

2 Choose carefully where to put the computer:
   * Don't put it where it will get too hot or cold.
   * Do not expose it to dust or smoke.
   * Avoid dampness or high humidity, which can cause short-circuits.
   * Make sure a power supply is nearby – trailing cables are dangerous.
   * Don't put it too near other electrical devices such as a hi-fi, TV or air-conditioning unit. These can generate strong magnetic fields which can affect the computer.

3 Protect the computer against surges in the power supply – fit a surge protector or line filter to the mains plug.

4 Find the serial number of the main unit. Write it down somewhere safe! You will need it if you have to contact the dealer for service or repair.

5 Find the ports on the back of the main unit. If they are labelled, for instance 'mouse', 'keyboard' and so on, you are in luck! If not, check the cables and see which fit – there is usually only one possibility. Sockets labelled COM1 and COM2 are for modems.

6 Connect the components in the following order:

- ✔ monitor
- ✔ mouse
- ✔ keyboard
- ✔ speakers (if separate)
- ✔ modem (if external)
- ✔ printer (for more information on how to do this, see page 40)

Starting up

1 Plug in the power cable and switch on both the processor and monitor. You should see a light on the main unit, and hear the cooling fan whirr into action.

2 The screen should show the computer starting its self-test routines. One of these should show how much RAM (memory) is fitted.

3 Finally the screen will show a desktop. What you see on a PC and a Mac will differ, but the basic idea is the same.

4 If you have a PC, run the mouse cursor over to the 'Start' box in the bottom left-hand corner and click. For a Mac, click on your hard disk icon. A menu or window will appear. Move the cursor to Programs or Applications on a Mac and a further menu or window will appear. If you click on any of these they will begin to run on your screen!

Icons and cursors

An icon is a small picture or symbol on the screen. When you move your mouse on its mat, you move a small arrow, or cursor, on the screen. By pointing the cursor at the icon, you can make a program run. Simply double-click (click the mouse twice) to start the program.

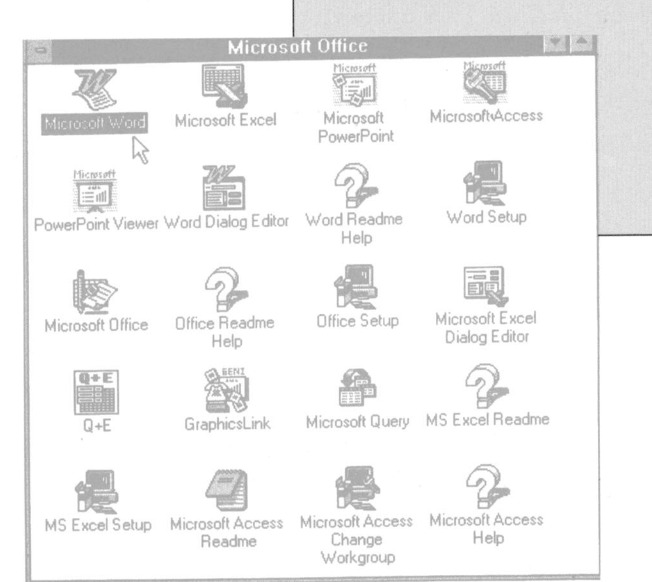

Turning off

Before you turn off the computer there are a few things to remember:

- Save the job you have been working on, by clicking on File, then Save or Save As (to give it a name).
- Close the program, or window, by clicking on File, then Close. YOU MUST CLOSE ALL PROGRAMS BEFORE SWITCHING OFF.
- Go to the Shut Down command, either in the File menu, the Start menu or the Special menu.
- If your computer tells you to wait before switching off, wait until it says it is safe to turn off the computer!

A COUPLE OF OTHER IMPORTANT TIPS:

✔ Don't leave the computer on permanently, because the electricity costs will be considerable.

✔ If you are not using the computer for a while, but are leaving it on, either turn the screen off OR set up a screensaver so that holding a still picture does not cause any problems.

Parent tip

"There is nearly always a simple reason if something goes wrong. The number of times that I've spent ages on the hotline trying to sort out a query, only to find that the computer's not plugged in!"

If it doesn't work

It is rare that computers completely 'crash'. Most difficulties can be caused by silly mistakes, like not turning the power on, or a cable being loose – so don't panic! A Mac and a PC will differ in the routines they use to check for problems. Most suppliers will have a 'hotline' you can contact if you need advice, but before you call

- Switch the computer off and turn the power off.
- Check that all the cables are in the right sockets.
- Try to turn the computer on again – it might go through a self-test routine. If it has fixed anything automatically, click OK if you are happy with it.
- If an error message appears, make a note of it and contact the supplier.

Buying Software

When you buy a computer it may have software loaded on to it. Your child's school will be using educational software. The more software you have, the more your computer can do. But what exactly is software?

- Hardware is the term for the machines – the computer, the printer or the speakers. If you can touch it or drop it, it's hardware!

- Software is the term for the programs which make the computer work. It also includes the applications such as word processing or games. Sometimes these come on small plastic disks which can be 'loaded' into the computer – these are called **floppy disks**. Often these floppy disks only work with either a PC or a Mac, so check. More and more they are being replaced by CD-ROMs and other types of equipment, which store more information.

HOW TO BUY

Software is not yet available as easily as books. Software costs much more, since one CD-ROM, for instance, can hold as much as a whole library of books. You also need to be clear about what you are buying, since you can't browse beforehand in the same way you can in a bookshop.

You can buy software through mail order, through some book clubs, and in computer shops. Ask your computer supplier where they would recommend – and always read the box carefully to make sure it will work on your computer!

Sources of advice

✔ Ask your friends and their children what they have enjoyed using.

✔ Join the Parents' Information Network (PIN). Their Family Membership gives you regular information about recommended software, as well as discounts on buying it. See the back of this book for further information.

Parent tip

"I had no idea what to buy, so I took recommendations from friends, and from a teacher at my child's school who knew about computers."

✔ Ask your child's teacher for recommendations. They may only know about school software – check if it will be suitable for home use before buying it. Bear in mind also that your child may be confused if you use school software at home differently from how the teacher uses it at school! Your child will certainly not want to repeat work done at school. There are many ways to learn and many games for the home market that are educational and will complement the work done at school.

✔ Read computer magazine reviews or look on the Internet. Try websites such as that of the UK government-run National Grid for Learning (www.ngfl.gov.uk) where you will often find experts' recommendations of good software.

Parent quote

"At first I found it very confusing, but then I looked at some reviews in a computer magazine and asked at the computer store, and it because far more simple!"

Types of software

Parent tip

"Always check the 'minimum specification' figures on the box. My computer was not really powerful enough to run the program I bought, and it showed!"

EDUCATIONAL

There is a wide range of educational software available, of varying quality. These programs can give children lots of practice in basic skills such as times tables and spelling. Some programs can teach a foreign language, using sounds as well as text and pictures.

Look for programs with several levels of difficulty, so that your child can progress from one level to the next. You can often set the starting level yourself, and you may also be able to control how much help your child is given by the program.

REFERENCE

Reference materials include encyclopaedias, atlases, dictionaries and resources covering such subjects as music and the human body. Most of these programs come on CD-ROMs so that text and illustrations can be combined. They might include pictures, graphics or video and sound clips which will bring the information alive. Your child can see and hear a volcano erupt, or travel through the human body!
The reference CD-ROMS can be 'searched' by typing in a word. The program will then show your child all the places in which that word occurs – very useful for specific homework projects! There will usually also be links to related information and how to find it.

Parent quote

"I thought the 'killing' games my child played were really mindless, so I tried one of the fun learning games, and it worked really well – great fun!"

GAMES AND FUN LEARNING

> **Parent tip**
>
> "If a new version of what you bought comes out, you can sometimes simply upgrade your old version to the standard of a new one – if you ask the supplier for the package. It saves buying the new one!"

Computer games are often the biggest attraction of a computer for a child, although they should not be their only use! The choice of games on offer is vast. They can range from one that requires the child to use his or her imagination to build a city of the future, to an adventure in which the child has to overcome as many enemies as possible. Most games will help improve a child's hand-eye co-ordination and mental agility, but this can obviously be outweighed by some antisocial effects! You must assess what sort of games you consider suitable for your child's enjoyment and development.

There are also now many programs which combine games with an educational element. For example, the child may take on a role – a pirate, perhaps. The pirate then has to solve problems or puzzles which require mathematical or logical skills. These can be an excellent compromise between the kinds of software used in school, and other games which the child might prefer to use!

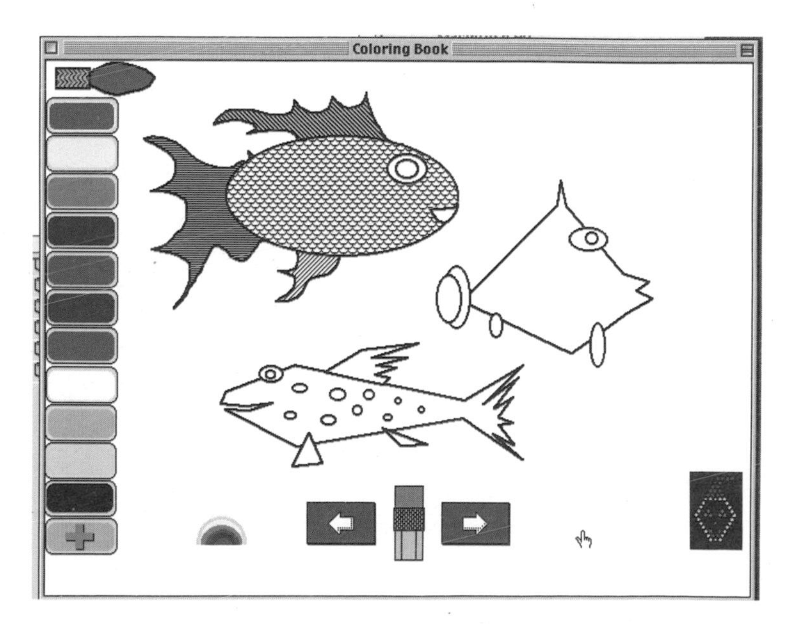

Getting started

The home computer can be used by the whole family, for everything from designing invitations to doing the accounts. A home computer will have different uses from one at work – it will probably contain more games and children's software, for a start!

Main uses for a home computer which complement work done at school might include:

- ✔ wordprocessing (e.g. Microsoft Word)
- ✔ spreadsheets (e.g. Microsoft Excel)
- ✔ databases (to store and organise information)
- ✔ design (called desktop publishing, using drawing or editing programs)
- ✔ email and Internet access
- ✔ fun learning games
- ✔ accessing information from CD-ROMS

Computers are being improved and updated all the time. It would be difficult (and expensive!) to keep up with these improvements, so don't worry if you have an old program – it will probably still be fine for your uses.

Get the most from your computer

Become familiar with your computer and find out what it can do.

Try using:

- the manuals you were given with the computer – although these are often written in technical language
- books with instructions – these can often be bought second-hand
- websites – some suggestions can be found at the back of this book
- the Help menu at the top of the screen. Check this whenever you're not sure!

Experiment and try things out! Computers are built to allow for this, so don't worry about making mistakes – your computer will warn you if you are about to lose anything. Practice is the best way to learn.

Wordprocessors

Wordprocessors are a step up from the old typewriters. For children and adults alike wordprocessors can make writing more enjoyable and more rewarding.

> **Parent quote**
>
> "My child was far more fearless than me when it came to trying things out on the computer. But nothing really went wrong."

- ✔ Work looks neat and professional.
- ✔ Words can be changed without the need to rewrite the whole text.
- ✔ Young children can record their ideas before they are skilled at forming letters.
- ✔ Spelling can be checked automatically.
- ✔ Work can be made attractive with special fonts in different sizes and colours.
- ✔ Diagrams drawn by the child, or special clip art, from the computer's memory, can be used to decorate the writing.

REMEMBER:

A computer is not a substitute for practising handwriting and spelling. These are still important skills.

KATIE

ANDY

Uses for wordprocessing will develop as a child progresses through school. Key Stage One children could be making badges (right) or name labels by incorporating pictures into their documents. Key Stage One pupils might try creating thank you letters and in Key Stage Two progress to longer stories, reports or simple magazine style articles combining drawings with text. Word processors can also be used for co-operative writing between two, three or four people. In a writing group children will learn a great deal from debating such things as plot, grammar and spelling. In addition they benefit socially from working together.

> **Parent tip**
>
> "Learn together with your child. We had fun telling each other new things we'd discovered!"

Some homework tasks, especially in Key Stage Two, might suggest that work be typed rather than written. This should be encouraged where a computer is available, but will not be a curriculum requirement. There are several good wordprocessing programs available. The more common ones are Word, WordPerfect, MSWorks and ClarisWorks. You might find it easiest to start your child on a program like Creative Writer or PenDown.

Parent tip

"Encourage your children to try creating labels for their cupboards and a name label for their bedroom door – it can be a good project to start on."

Creating and saving documents

To create a new document, click on File and then New! When you have finished what you are doing, you need to save it under a name, using Save As (also in the File Menu). Once your child has written a story or letter on screen, he or she will want to save it and print it out. Each piece of writing is called a document.

A child will need to learn how to find and retrieve documents. This is done using the Open command or icon. The document can be changed and then saved again by clicking on Save. Your computer will give you instructions and remind you when a document has not been saved.

Editing a document

Parent quote

"After years of nagging, it was the wordprocessor that finally got my child to do thank you letters. She can save a format with pictures, then change the details every time – far easier!"

To change any piece of writing, you need to select it (so the computer knows what to change). This is done by highlighting the words or sentences: put the cursor at the start and drag the mouse to the end of the text you want, whilst holding down the button on the mouse.

Deleting a piece of writing:

- highlight the part you want to delete
- press the Delete key on the keyboard

Copying a piece of writing:

- highlight the part you want to copy
- point the arrow at the Copy icon and click the mouse
- move the cursor to where you want the selected writing to be copied
- point the arrow at the Paste icon and click

Moving a piece of writing:

- highlight the part you want to move
- point the arrow at the Cut icon and click
- move the cursor to where you want to put the writing
- click on the Paste icon

REMEMBER:

If you hold the cursor over an icon WITHOUT clicking for a couple of seconds, an explanation box will tell you what the icon does.

You can select the number of icons on your screen when you work by going to the View menu and then Toolbars.

Printing a document

There are two ways to print what you are working on:

✔If you want to print all of the document immediately, click on the Print icon.

✔If you only want to print certain pages, or make several copies, go to File and Print and you can select exactly which pages and how many of them you want to print.

Setting up your printer

Simply plugging in your printer will not necessarily make it work automatically. Your computer will not recognise your printer unless you tell it what sort of printer it is. To do this:

- Go to the Printer menu, which will either be in the Start menu under Settings, or in Chooser, or have an icon of its own – depending on your computer. If you are not sure, check with the supplier or instruction manual.

- Double click on the icon that says Add Printer.

- Follow the instructions, pressing Next when you have completed a box.

- The computer will ask if you want the new printer to be your default printer. If you want to print everything automatically from there, say yes!

Spreadsheets

A spreadsheet is a table of boxes (cells) created by a computer. For a child this resembles the squared paper he or she uses in school for vertical sums and block graphs or bar charts.

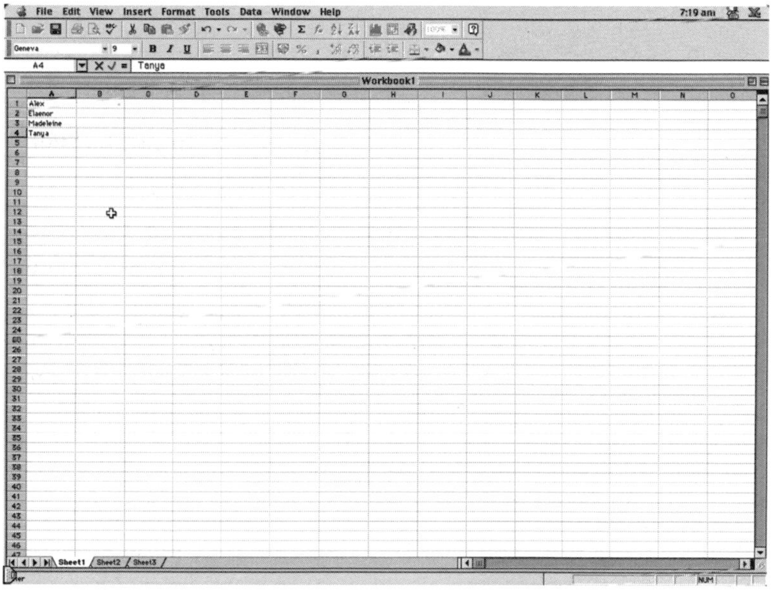

Terms to use when working with spreadsheets:

Column:

This is the vertical information. Each cell has an address made up of the letter of the column and the number of the row.

Row:

This is the horizontal information.

Cell:

This is the small box containing an individual piece of information.

Formula bar:

This is the bar below the line of icons and above the table itself. It tells you what is in the highlighted cell.

Letters, numbers and words can be inserted into any cell and, with appropriate commands, the computer will handle them in a variety of ways. Your child will learn to use spreadsheets to:

- ✔ add up and sort numbers
- ✔ calculate an average from a range of numbers
- ✔ sort words alphabetically
- ✔ present a table of words and numbers
- ✔ create graphs from a table of numbers and letters

By Year 3 children are solving problems by organising and interpreting numerical data. The primary school subjects which have most to gain from the use of spreadsheets are probably science and maths. In maths they can be used for early work in algebra. Children often use complicated numbers (data) in scientific or mathematical investigations. The difficulty of handling that data can make it harder for children to understand the maths or science. Spreadsheets help by reducing the need for children to struggle with calculations, ordering or graphing.

Older children can make even more use of spreadsheets. For example, a class might investigate the different ingredients of breakfast cereals. They could compare four types of cereal and create a spreadsheet for their data, showing the amount of each of the main food types. The teacher could help to design the spreadsheet, or the children could do it all themselves.

Spreadsheets should not be a way of 'shortcutting' homework (children, for instance, should still do their own tables, sums and graphs when required), but they can be a useful tool. They can be a visual example of how to find co-ordinates (for pupils in Year 6). They also enable children to present their work in a smart and colourful way.

Creating and editing a spreadsheet

Spreadsheets are as easy to open, print and save as any other document. However, spreadsheets are organised in a different way from other documents: instead of being in pages, they are in sheets which can group together into a workbook.

Parent tip

"We do not have a computer at home, but I always ask my child to help me look things up, like street names in the map, and entries in the encyclopaedia. That way he learns how information can be organised."

Spreadsheets are very powerful and they have thousands of uses for the computer expert – but there are only a few which your child will need to know:

CREATING A TABLE OF DATA:

- fill in horizontal and vertical axes, probably down column A and along row 1
- click on the cells to put in the data
- double click on the cell to change the data inside

HOW TO ADD THE AMOUNTS IN A TABLE:

- select the column or row containing the amounts you want to add by dragging the cursor across the cells.
- add as many rows and columns together as you like.
- click the Add icon, and all the amounts will be added

CREATING A SIMPLE GRAPH

- select the cells which contain the information you want in the graph
- click on the Chart Wizard icon
- follow the instructions, pressing Next when you have made each choice
- you have a graph! This can be moved into any other program (such as a wordprocessing program) using the Cut, Copy and Paste icons

Databases

Databases are collections of information. Your address book is a relatively small database compared with the giant database offered by a telephone directory or the information that a computer can store. Computers can look through database entries and check any part of a database very rapidly.

BRANCHING DATABASES

One of the most common ways to introduce children to databases is through a branching database. This type of database relies on questions to divide a set of objects into two smaller sets. Once it is complete, other children can use this branching database to identify any object. Later, in the Key Stage Two school, older children will use databases like this to enter information about the birds, minibeasts and plants they are studying. This encourages them to look closely at the items they want to sort and spot similarities and differences.

A branching database of pets might look like this:

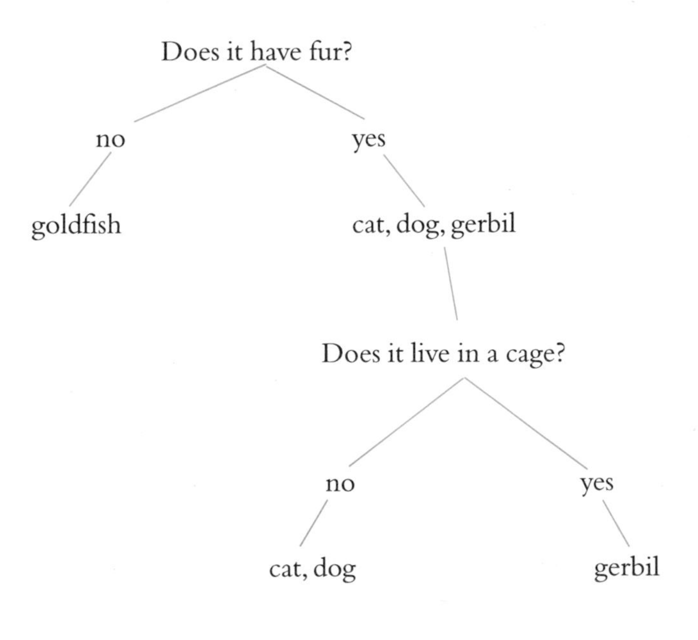

Your child in Key Stage One will be learning to use I.C.T. to save data and access stored information. In Key Stage Two pupils will learn to add to, amend and investigate stored information. Simple databases can be an ideal source of ideas. Many schools have begun to compile a database of their reading and information books so that children can search for a book which meets their needs. In science they may collect personal information about their classmates and, with Sort and Filter facilities, find out, for example, whether more boys than girls are left-handed, or what the most popular colour is.

USEFUL TERMS FOR WORKING WITH DATABASES

Your child may need the correct technical vocabulary for retrieving information, in this case about a restaurant:

Record	all the information about one restaurant
File	a collection of all the records. This file might be called Eating Places
Field	one of the categories of information, such as the name of the restaurant, or whether it has parking
Sort	a command which allows you to sort the information in one field, so that you could sort Indian restaurants, for example, from other styles of cooking
Filter	this allows you to sort through one or more fields and check whether one record is equal to, less than or more than another. For example, you could find out which restaurants charge more than others for the same thing!

The Internet

You have heard of it, but are perhaps not sure exactly what it is! The Internet can be thought of as a worldwide library and telephone exchange joining together computers around the world. The computers belong to governments, universities, companies, organisations and individuals. The Internet is growing all the time. People use the Internet for many different purposes:

- finding information
- sending messages (email)
- sharing computer software
- socialising

It is not essential to have Internet access, but it is a useful tool. If you can connect to the Internet, you can find as much information as you need on any subject, as long as you know how. More and more children will be asked if they have access to the Internet to find information, perhaps for a school project or to extend their interest in a subject. It is possible to use the Internet in cyber cafés (cafés where you pay for an hour's use of all the facilities needed to access the Internet), or even in large toystores. This can be a good way of testing it out before paying for a connection!

You and your child – using the Internet

Here are some examples of how you and your child might use the Internet together:

✔ sending a message to friends or school

✔ finding information on a subject for a homework project

✔ finding out what is going on in the local area

✔ finding suggestions for computer software to buy

✔ keeping up-to-date with a favourite singer or team

What is the Web?

The Web is short for the World Wide Web, which is shortened in the 'address' of an Internet site to www. The Web consists of thousands of websites. Each website is made up of web pages like a series of magazine pages, usually with pictures as well as text. A school, for example, may have a website with pages containing the prospectus, the holiday dates, pictures of children's work – and even the homework for this week!

Most companies and organisations have websites. You can move from one site to another by following links between them. For instance, if you 'log on' to a site which belongs to a travel company, it will not only contain information about holidays, but will have links to British Airways or Railtrack so that you can easily jump to information held on their sites.

What is email?

When you join the Internet, you will be able to get an email address. This is an electronic mailbox which enables you to send messages to other people with mailboxes. You can send words, pictures and even sounds in your emails. When someone sends you an email it arrives in your mailbox. When you log on to the Internet you can open your mailbox and read your messages.

The great advantage of email is its speed. You can send a message to anywhere in the world almost instantly. In comparison to this, normal mail is so slow it has been called 'snail-mail'. Email is even quicker than faxing for sending documents (which can then be printed off by the person who receives them).

The person to whom the message is being sent

Ways of storing all the messages

You can send other people copies of the same message

The message

This picture shows a typical email system. Remember: there are many email systems available. They all lool very different, but what they do is the same.

What is a browser?

A browser is the main piece of software you need to be able to see web pages on your computer. Browsers are usually FREE and are often installed on new machines. The two main browsers are Microsoft Explorer and Netscape Navigator.

How do I get connected to the Internet?

Most computers will be built to accommodate Internet connection. There are a few basic essentials you need to have. Most of these will already be built into your computer.

CHECK YOUR COMPUTER HAS:

- at least 8Mb of RAM (memory – stated when you turn on your computer)
- about 800 Mb of free hard disk space
- a processor with a speed of 486 MHz or faster

YOU WILL ALSO NEED:

- a modem (either already built in internally, or fitted on externally)
- email software (probably available from your supplier, or built in)
- a browser (see page 48)
- a video card (check with your supplier about this)

A sound card and speakers will also be helpful but are not essential. Finally, you need to set up an account with an Internet service provider (ISP). You can usually dial into the ISP through the same channels (and for the same cost) as a local call.

What is a modem?

A modem is a box which changes computer signals into signals to send along your telephone line. They either plug into the computer or are fitted inside. Either way, they will have a cable which connects the computer to the ordinary telephone socket in the wall (Remember: if you use your normal telephone socket, you can't receive any phone calls while you're on the Internet! It is common to get another telephone socket fitted specifically for the computer).

The speed of the modem is measured in Kilobits per second (Kbps). You will need a modem of at least 28.8 Kbps in order to access the Internet at a reasonable speed.

Internet Service Providers

The Internet Service Provider (ISP) connects computers to the Internet. When you have an account with an ISP it will 'recognise' your computer when you connect, enabling you to use the Internet. There are more and more companies offering this service, and two main considerations to distinguish between them:

DO I HAVE TO PAY?

Some ISPs charge a reasonable monthly fee. You will usually be charged via credit card. In these cases it is worth seeing what you get for your money! Other ISPs are free but may not offer the same services.

DOES THE ISP OFFER AN INFORMATION SERVICE?

Some ISPs provide useful information – for instance on the weather, travel and sport – on its sites. There are even ISPs now specifically concerned with education.

Other ISPs simply act as a kind of gateway to the Internet.

DO I GET UNLIMITED TIME FOR MY MONTHLY CHARGE?

If you are paying the ISP a monthly charge, it may be a fixed rate, in which case you can have unlimited time 'online' (using the Internet) during that month. Remember – you will also be paying for the local rate 'telephone calls' when you are connected!

Alternatively you may just be charged for your actual time online.

WHAT TECHNICAL SUPPORT DOES THE ISP OFFER?

Some ISPs have helplines. If they do, check when it is available. If you are most likely to be using the Internet in the evenings and at the weekend you need to make sure there will be someone there to answer your call!

If the helpline for the ISP uses a premium rate line – often the case with cheaper companies – you could be paying a lot for help.

HOW LARGE IS THE COMPANY?

You may have difficulties logging on if your ISP is small. Small companies can only cope with a certain number of people trying to log on at the same time.

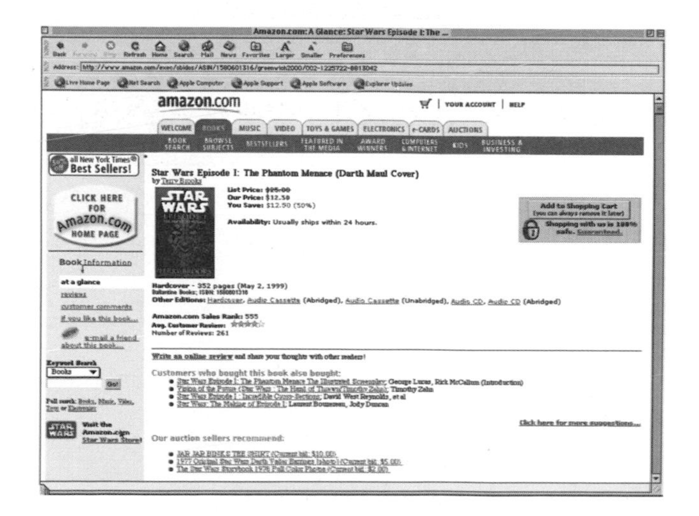

Surfing the Web

The main problem with the Internet is that it is easy to get lost – not surprising, considering its vastness. If you know exactly what you are looking for, it will save you considerable amounts of time. But even if you don't, there are ways of reaching your destination, probably finding new unexpected surprises on the way. First of all, you need to log on.

LOGGING ON

- Check your modem is plugged into your telephone socket.
- Doubleclick on the icon for your browser program (such as Microsoft Explorer or Netscape Navigator).
- Click on 'Connect'.
- Your modem is now dialling. You may hear some funny sounds when the computer at the other end answers.
- Your screen will change and you will see a moving symbol in one corner. You are now connected!

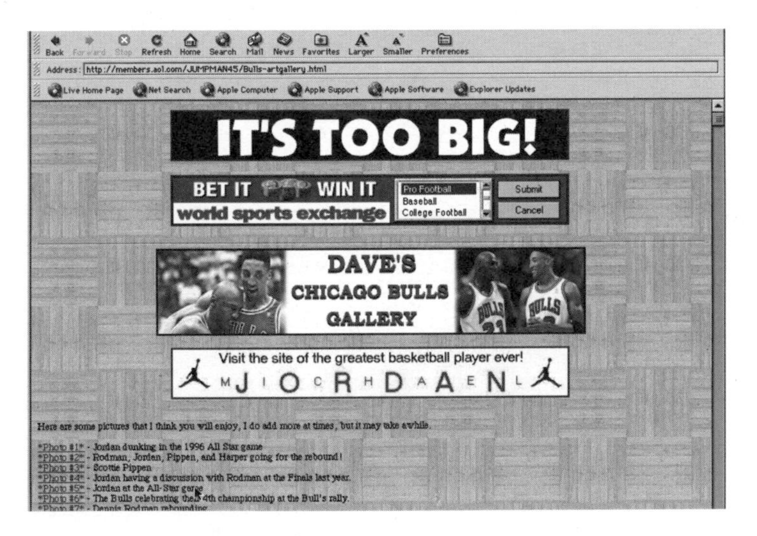

A typical webpage will look something like this. Buttons are used to move around the Web.

Now you need to find what you're looking for …

FINDING A WEBSITE

Each website has an address (sometimes called a URL) which usually has 'www' in it. For example, www.lettsed.co.uk is the Letts Educational website.

If you know the address already, the website will be easy to find. Type the address into the address bar at the top of the screen. Make sure you have typed it correctly, and it doesn't have any capital letters. Press Enter and the first page of the website will open.

Many websites have a page of links to other parts of the site or related sites. These links are underlined or shown in a different colour. Your cursor will probably change shape (for instance, to a pointing finger) if you place it on a link. Click on the link and it will 'jump' to that new page. You are now surfing!

If you get lost, you can always retrace your steps by clicking on the 'back' button at the top of the screen.

Your child will often want to find information without knowing exactly where to start looking. Most of the time he or she will know the topic – rainbows, perhaps, or Australia – but not where to go first. This is when search engines are useful. Your ISP will probably have a search engine on its main website, but there are many different search engines available. Not all of these can connect to all the websites on the Internet, so it is a good idea to use more than one search engine when gathering information.

HOW TO USE A SEARCH ENGINE

Click on the Search button at the top of the screen. This will connect you to a choice of search engines which will ask you for key words or phrases. Try to be as exact as you can.

You will be given a list of results: links with brief descriptions of what each site contains. This means you can select the most relevant sites.

It is sometimes best to go directly to a large search engine, such as www.altavista.com or www.yahoo.co.uk. Here you can try typing in questions, such as 'What is the tallest mountain?' or 'Where can I find information on the National Curriculum?'. The most relevant sites should appear first.

There are several sites and search engines specifically designed for children's use. For example, Mirago (www.mirago.co.uk/zone) is a directory that has been filtered for use by children. If your child wants to find out about something not listed, he or she can type a word into the search box, and a list of related sites will appear, with the most relevant at the top. For more useful sites see the Useful information at the end of this book.

The Web provides a huge illustrated library from around the world, and can be very useful for homework. But you will need to show your child how to select carefully from the information available. A printout of all the information on Egyptian mummies, for instance, might not help, but finding a labelled picture of one could be ideal. Remember that the Internet is a tool to supplement class work – a quick print out is not a substitute for a child putting more creative thought into his or her homework!

Parent tips

"Give children a time limit surfing the Web, or they can be on there for hours – and it can get expensive!"

"Some large sites have really useful maps in them, which my child found helpful in understanding how the whole thing fits together."

Safety first

There are many safety concerns surrounding the Internet and particularly its use by children. There are indeed thousands of 'adult sites' on the Web, which children are unlikely to find by accident – but it is worth being aware of the danger. There are also numerous 'chatrooms' where children could end up giving up personal information, or be drawn into uncomfortable conversations.

Remember that the Internet is not intrinsically unsafe, either to your child, or your computer – as long as you use it properly.

Children and the Internet

Parents have two main concerns about their children using the Internet are:

- that they might stumble upon sites containing explicit sexual or violent material

- that they might be able to 'chat' with strangers who may or may not be safe

A basic rule, especially for young children, is to keep the computer in a place where you can see what they are doing. It is not advisable, for instance, to allow a child Internet access in his or her bedroom.

Safe Internet use

SOFTWARE SAFETY

There are now programs you can buy which allow you to control which websites your children can access. Cyberpatrol, Netnanny and Netsurf are some examples. These work by blocking access to sites containing certain words – you set the limits by choosing these words. Your browser software may also be able to do this – look in the instruction manual for details, or ask your supplier.

You may decide to test some software – a game, for instance – before you let your child use it if you are concerned about its content.

SAFETY IN RULES

It is advisable to establish a few rules for your child to know before they surf the Web. The suggestions on this page are provided courtesy of the National Center for Missing and Exploited Children, and can be learned by a child. They will make sure that the Internet remains a safe place for children to go, and reinforce the message that parents must be involved in their child's Internet use.

Rules

- I will not give out personal information, such as my address, telephone number, parents' work address or phone number or the name and location of my school, without my parents' permission.
- I will tell my parents right away if I come across any information that makes me feel uncomfortable.
- I will never agree to get together with someone I 'meet' online without first checking with my parents. If my parents agree to the meeting, I will be sure that it is in a public place and bring my mother or father along.
- I will never send a person my picture or anything else without first checking with my parents.
- I will not respond to any messages that are mean or make me feel uncomfortable. It is not my fault if I get a message like that and if I do, I will tell my parents right away so that they can contact the online service.
- I will talk with my parents so that we can set up rules for going online. We will decide upon the time of day I can be online, and appropriate areas for me to visit. I will not access other areas or break these rules without their permission.

Email security

Email is generally a secure form of communication, but there are some guidelines children should learn.

- Never give your email address to anyone you are unsure about – this includes companies.

- Remember that people can hide behind any identity when using email. They may not be who they seem!

- You don't have to answer an email.

- Don't include your address or telephone number in messages to strangers.

Viruses

A virus is a rogue program designed to damage the computer. It can only enter your computer from outside – that is, from the Internet or email. Many websites enable you to copy programs or files from a site onto your computer – this is downloading. There is a small danger that a virus will be hidden in what you download. If the virus is hidden, it could remove all the programs from your computer, damage the screen, or stop the computer from working (but this is very unusual).

Parent quote

"Don't worry overly about the Internet and all the horrors that you hear about on it. As long as you keep an eye on your child, she or he is unlikely to access any bad sites."

GUIDELINES TO HELP AVOID VIRUSES

- Never download software if you are at all unsure about its source.

- If you want to check something before you put it on your computer, save it onto a disk (slot a floppy disk into the computer, and Save in Drive:A). It can be checked on here without putting the computer at risk.

- To check any software use an anti-virus program, which may be included when you buy the computer, or can be bought separately.

- Emails sometimes contain files as well as messages. These are called **attachments** and have little icons within the emails. Treat these in the same way as software, by saving them onto a disk first.

- As a general rule, if you receive an email attachment with .exe at the end (for example virus.exe), do not open it at all, particularly if you do not know where it is from.

Seven tips for working on I.C.T. with your child

1. Enjoy learning with and from your child.
2. Have the confidence to 'have a go'.
3. The basics of reading, writing and maths are vital – computers can assist, but should never be seen as a replacement for traditional ways of learning.
4. Find out how your child is using I.C.T. in school. Ask the school to hold an information evening
5. Let your child progress with I.C.T. at his or her own pace – and try to keep up yourself!
6. Take the necessary security precautions with Internet access – surf with your child.
7. Remember that technology is changing all the time. Move with it!

Glossary

Attachments Files that can come attached to an email and accessed be from there.

Attainment targets Targets for what children are expected to do in each subject at different stages. Each attainment target is divided into eight levels, like steps up a ladder.

Baseline Assessment Teacher observation of children within the first seven weeks of entering the Reception class, which is used to assess learning levels in maths, English and social skills.

Browser The main piece of software needed to see web pages on your computer. Usually freely installed on new machines.

CD-ROM A CD which can be loaded into your computer and contains words, images and sound.

Ceefax The information service available in text form on most television sets.

Chat room A way of 'chatting' to people over the Internet, by sending messages back and forth.

Concept keyboards Keyboards with large shapes, words or numbers for children to use to enhance their learning at a young age.

Core subjects The main subjects in the National Curriculum: English, maths and science. R.E. (religious education) and I.C.T. (Information and Communications Technology) are also treated like core subjects. These are the only subjects where set Programmes of Study have to be taught in full.

Cursor The arrow or cross on your screen which points to icons and words to make commands, and is manipulated by moving the mouse.

Cyber cafe A café where customers use the Internet.

Database An electronic way of organising and storing information, like a card index system.

Desktop The screen as it appears when you turn on your computer.

Desktop publishing The term for designing and changing images and layouts on a screen.

Digital camera A special camera which acts like a video camera and can transfer photos onto the computer.

Download The process which moves software or information from a disk, a CD or the Internet on to your computer.

Drives The parts into which your hard disk is divided: 'A' drive will usually indicate the information on a floppy disk; 'C' drive is where most of your personal work is likely to be stored, although you can choose.

Email Electronic mail, sent via the Internet.

Floppy disk A plastic disk containing information which can be loaded into a drive in your computer. Work can be saved on a floppy disk.

Foundation subjects Subjects covered in schools as part of the National Curriculum which are not English, maths and science (the core subjects) or R.E. and I.C.T. These include history, geography, music, design technology, art and P.E..

Hard disk The part of the computer which stores all the programs you use and the work you do.

Hardware The machines that make up the computer.

Icon A small image or picture on your screen – if you click on an icon you will command whatever it means to happen!

ILS Integrated learning systems.

Information and Communications Technology (I.C.T.) The term to replace I.T. (Information Technology), meaning the use of computers and other electronic means to enhance learning.

Internet The service which connects computers around the world, creating a 'web' of information and communication facilities that can be accessed.

Internet Service Provider (ISP) The service which connects computers to the Internet. When you have an account with an ISP it will recognise your computer when you connect, enabling you to use the Internet.

Joystick A piece of equipment, like a gear stick, which is attached to the computer and used for moving objects in games.

Key Stages The stages at which a child's education can be assessed, after following a Programme of Study. There are four Key Stages, dividing ages 5-7, 7-11, 11-14 and 14-16.

LEA (Local Education Authority) The city, county, borough or district education authority. LEAs have many specific roles – especially in admissions, finance and special educational needs.

Link A way of jumping from one website to another on the Internet.

Literacy Hour The time each day which schools have to devote to teaching literacy skills.

Logo The computer language used to control a turtle.

Mac Apple Macintosh computer.

Menu A list of options on your computer screen.

Modem This connects your computer to the telephone line so that you can use the Internet.

Monitor The screen on your computer.

Mouse The attachment to the computer used to point to commands and click.

Multimedia The all-inclusive term for computer applications which involves sound and images, such as videos or the Internet.

National Curriculum The government's system of education broken into four Key Stages, which applies to all pupils of compulsory school age in maintained schools. It contains core and foundation (non-core) subjects, and incorporates National Tests at the end of each Key Stage.

OFSTED (Office for Standards in Education) The government department which oversees inspections and sends teams to assess individual schools.

Paint A program enabling a child to play on screen with colours, patterns and shapes.

PC A personal computer.

Port The hole in the case of the computer into which a cable for a peripheral will fit.

Processor The part of a computer which controls its actions, operating at a particular speed (MHz).

Program A general term for a piece of software or an application which works on your computer.

RAM The memory of the computer (the amount it can hold to work with).

Scanner This copies pictures or words and transfers them onto your screen.

Screensaver An automatic moving display on the screen when the screen is inactive and not being used.

Search engine An Internet site or service which searches for a site containing the words you provide.

Sheets These can be placed on a concept keyboard to help children learn basic skills.

Software The term for programs which make the computer work. It also includes the applications such as wordprocessing or games. It can be bought and loaded onto your computer.

Specification The type of computer parts (speed, make etc.).

Spreadsheet A computer grid system which allows the manipulation of numbers and words, and can be used by your child to create graphs and tables.

Surfing Exploring the Internet, following links to jump from one site to the next.

Surge protector This is sometimes called a line filter. It is a special kind of plug which prevents surges in electricity from reaching your computer.

Teletext The information service available in text form on most television sets.

Turtle A robot that can be controlled and made to move backwards, forwards and sideways. Mainly used by Key Stage One children.

URL An Internet 'address'.

Virus A program which can enter your computer from an external source, usually an attachment or some downloaded software, and can destroy data and programs.

Web The World Wide Web is a collection of websites containing words, sounds and images.

Windows The system used for the display on modern PCs and Macs.

Wizard The term used in some computer programs for a 'magic' way of carrying out a task, in the form of step by step instructions based on a template.

Wordprocessing The manipulation of text, and sometimes images, on the computer.

USEFUL INFORMATION

Advisory Centre for Education (ACE)
Department A, Unit 1B Aberdeen Studios,
22 Highbury Grove, London N5 2DQ
Web: www.ace-ed.org.uk
Phone: 020 7354 8321
Free advice, information and support for parents of children in state schools.

The Advisory Unit on Computers in Education
Web: www.advisory-unit.org.uk
Phone: 01707 266 714
Fax: 01707 273 684
Offers advice, training and information on the use of I.C.T. to support pupils who have learning difficulties.

Basic Skills Agency
7th Floor, Commonwealth House,
1-19 New Oxford Street, London WC1A 1NU
Web: www.basic-skills.co.uk
Phone: 020 7405 4017
National development agency for basic literacy and numeracy skills.

DfEE (Department for Education and Employment)
Sanctuary Buildings, Great Smith Street,
London SW1P 3BT
Web: www.dfee.gov.uk
Phone: 020 7925 5555

National Association for Special Educational Needs
NASEN House, 4/5 Amber Business Village,
Amber Close, Amington, Tamworth B77 4RP
Web: www.nasen.org.uk
Phone: 01827 311 500

National Confederation for Parent Teacher Associations (NCPTA)
2 Ebbsfleet Estate, Stonebridge Road,
Gravesend, Kent DA11 9DZ
Web: www.rmplc.co.uk/orgs/ncpta
Phone: 01474 560 618
Promotes partnership between home and school, children, parents, teachers and education authorities.

SOFTWARE

Parent's Information Network (PIN)
PO Box 1577, London W7 3ZT
PIN is an independent organisation set up to help parents become more informed and confident with computers. It provides reviews and information on software, starter packs for parents setting up a computer and knowing what to buy, guidance on using the Web, and recommended sites.
Web: www.pin-parents.com
Email: editor@pin-parents.com

There are more and more varieties of educational software becoming available. Below are some suggestions to explore.

www.stormeducational.co.uk
www.ppsoft.demon.co.uk
www.educational.co.uk
www.cambridgelearning.com
www.webcit.co.uk/3c

OTHER PUBLICATIONS

On the Internet and Internet Safety
There is a 16 page leaflet to help schools with their Internet access policy, summarising the issues involved. Produced by the National Association for Advisors for Computers in Education (NAACE) it is called 'Promoting the Responsible Use of the Internet in Schools', Web: www.bcs.org.uk/ial.html